GENERAL LEE

AND

SANTA CLAUS

GENERAL LEE

AND

SANTA CLAUS

MRS. LOUISE CLACK'S

Christmas Gifts to her little Southern Friends.

GUILD BINDERY PRESS

General Lee and Santa Claus

Printed in the United States of America

ISBN 1-55793-106-2

Guild Bindery Press wishes to acknowledge the Virginia
Historical Society and the Robert E. Lee Memorial
Association for their support in the republication of this
book.

A royalty from the sale of this book is
donated to Stratford Hall, birthplace of
Robert E. Lee

General Lee and Santa Claus as well as other Guild Bindery Press
titles may be purchased at special discounts for fund-raising,
educational or sales promotion use. Contact Guild Bindery Press,
Inc. Post Office Box 38099, Memphis, Tennessee 38183 / 901-758-
8577 or 1-800-622-7936.

First printing
5   4   3   2   1

Guild Bindery Press
Post Office Box 38099
Germantown, Tennessee 38183
(901) 758-8577
1-800-622-7936

General Lee and Santa Claus

I N T R O D U C T I O N

General Robert E. Lee's surrender at Appomattox in 1865 effectively ended
the Civil War and began a difficult, decades-long process of healing, as the
American South came to grips with its defeat. Out of the region's mood of
despair appeared a body of literature that brought about the apotheosis of
Robert E. Lee, glorifying him as the Southern ideal. By the turn of the century,
the American people perceived Lee as a symbol of the enduring gentility and
dignity of the South, as well as the foremost representative of national reconciliation.

Originally appearing in 1867, Louise Clack's General Lee and Santa Claus fully
anticipates the unique position destined for Lee in the pantheon of our national
heroes. Clack's work emphasizes Lee's exemplary character in much the same
way as works written half a century later, such as Hamilton's The Life of
Robert E. Lee for Boys and Girls (1917).

General Lee and Santa Claus is doubly remarkable for both its pairing of these
unlikely partners in a children's book and its portrayal of Lee as the mediator
of Confederate defeat during his own lifetime. Finding Lee depicted in this
context in a work published before his death in 1870 is highly unusual. With
the exception of General Lee and Santa Claus, the remaking of Lee's image and
his transformation from rebel general to national icon is a phenomenon almost
wholly confined to the decades after he died.

The rediscovery of such a historically significant artifact is, indeed, thrilling.
Yet, General Lee and Santa Claus is also enjoyable on the level intended by its
author—as a timeless Christmas story with a special appeal to children. The
narrative is centered around the request (asked of General Lee), "Please tell us
whether Santa Claus loves the little rebel children, for we think he doesn't;
because he did not come to see us for four Christmas Eves." Featuring a trio of
fantastic dreams, it is structurally reminiscent of the ghostly visitations in
Charles Dickens' "A Christmas Carol"—a story which strongly influences our
celebration of the holiday season even today.

Randall Bedwell

O C T O B E R   1 9 9 6

CHRISTMAS EVE AND CHRISTMAS MORN.

THE bright fire is beaming,
The silver urn steaming,
  Now give them all,
Dear father, and mother,
And sister, and brother,
  A cheerful call.

See they come clustering,
Each softly flustering,
  Around the board;
Waiting most patiently,
For blessing said sapiently,
  Of Holy Word.

3

CHRISTMAS EVE AND CHRISTMAS MORN.

Now the spoons rattle,
All begin to prattle,
   Just hear the glee;
Hot cakes and muffins rare,
Sweetmeats and waffles there,
   Coffee and tea.

Merrily laughs papa,
Cheerfully smiles mamma,
   Glad mirth resounds;
Even Rover wags his tail,
(Mind you he'd never fail)
   As in he bounds.

Ended the merry meal,
All to mamma appeal,
   For music sweet.
She, with good will, complies,
While all with sparkling eyes,
   Spring to their feet.

4

CHRISTMAS EVE AND CHRISTMAS MORN.

Bright looks the parlor floor;
Wide stands the open door;
　　Take a peep there.
Father's cigar bring; quick,
Don't mind the curtains, Dick,
　　Mother don't care.

See the gay dancers,
Grouped for the lancers,
　　Ready for sport;
Now they glide lightly,
While she touches sprightly,
　　The pianoforte.

Laughing and rolicking,
Sporting and frolicking,
　　Dancing is o'er.
Readings poetical,
Comic, pathetical,
　　Take up an hour.

Now they must cease their play,
For, to their great dismay,
Bed-time has come.
Dear father and mother,
Draw near one another,
In the hushed room.

Speak of their daily cares,
Each of them unawares
Of aught but love;
And with looks sadly mild,
Of their dear spirit child,
In heaven above.

Now, they to rest have gone,
And see across the lawn,
Santa Claus hies;
Straight for the roof he makes,
Hark how the nursery quakes,
As down he flies.

See him now peering,
Grinning, and leering,
   At each little face;
But he don't mean to harm,
Nor even to alarm,
   One in the place.

Quick he begins to fill,
Stockings with right good will,
   For girls and boys.
Dolls, soldiers, ribbons bright,
Oh! 'tis a goodly sight,
   To see the toys.

Up then he speeds away,
And in the East the day
   Breaks into morn.
Shout, little children, shout,
Ring your glad voices out,
   A Saviour is born.

On the first Christmas day,
Many long years away,
   The Holy Child
Waked in his manger bed,
Held up his little head,
   Blessed God and smiled.

And with that smile, a prayer,
Rose on the hallowed air,
   Children for ye:
That on all Christmas days,
Joyful might be your praise,
   Joyful and free.

So, little children, shout,
Ring your glad voices out,
   A Saviour is born.
Happy, most happy be,
God blessed the day to ye,
   The first Christmas morn.

Lutie, Birdie and Minnie,

A STORY ABOUT THREE LITTLE SOUTHERN GIRLS.

N the pleasantest portions of one of our best Southern States live three little girls, whose names are Lutie, Birdie and Minnie. Lutie and Birdie are sisters, and Minnie is their cousin.

Lutie and Birdie have no mother, but a grandma, and a father, and an' auntie. Their mother went away to heaven before our great national trouble came upon us, for she was too pure and holy for the heavy trials of this wicked earth; so God, who is ever good, took her to a blessed country, where sorrow never goes; and now she sits at Jesus' feet, with a pure white lily in her hand, and a halo about her head, and day and night she prays for her dear ones on earth, that they may be made worthy of the promises of Christ.

It is a great benefit to have a dear mother in heaven—do you not think so, my little readers? I know it seems very hard when our friends are first removed there; but, oh! what an inestimable privilege it is to have one of our own family safe at Jesus' feet, and ever watching over and praying for us, and directing the dear Lord's attention to us particularly.

And thus it is with little Lutie and Birdie. They have an angel mother at Jesus' feet; and she is more able to protect them there, than when she clasped their little hands in hers on earth.

I wish all my little Southern readers knew my little pets; but, as most of them cannot, I will have to try and describe them. Lutie is a fine sturdy child of nine years of age, as plump and rosy as a ripe cherry, and as serious most of the time as a lady of forty. She is very studious for the sake of learning itself, and is seldom seen without a book in her hand.

She loves particularly to read stories of the ancient gods and goddesses, and it is very funny sometimes to hear her allusions to these mythical characters; for she does not always pronounce their names according to Greek and Latin rule ; but, when we laugh at her for this, she takes it very good-naturedly, and asks for the proper pronunciation, and afterwards always uses it.

Birdie, the younger sister, is a bright little elf, but does not like books at all, and would much rather play with dolls all day than to read even fairy tales. Her true name is not Birdie—that is only a nick-name ; but she was so like a little bereft birdling when her dear mother was taken away to heaven, which was when she was only a few weeks old, that this name has clung to her, and she will always be " our Birdie."

Both Lutie and Birdie have auburn hair and sparkling dark brown eyes, and Birdie's eyes see more than anyone else's eyes.

Last, but not least, comes bright-browed, blue-eyed Minnie. She is another little elf like Birdie, only perhaps a little more elfish. She can run, dance, play and be mischievous quicker than any child I ever saw ; but, with her mischief, she is so good-natured that it is very hard to get angry with her, especially when she holds up her tiny mouth for a kiss after her pranks, and promises to be ever so good for the future.

By nature she has a very pious little heart, and sometimes she will stop her play, and go by herself and say her prayers. She loves blue and green better than any other colors; and when you ask her why, she says because God uses those colors most.

One day she was sitting on the piazza with Lutie and Birdie. She had dressed her pet cat in one of her doll's dresses, and was trying to rock her to sleep. It was a lovely day, and the birds were singing very gaily. Suddenly, Minnie ceased singing to the cat, and exclaimed, " Oh! oh! oh! I have just found out why the birds sing so much more beautifully than people do. It is because they fly so near to heaven that they catch the voices of the angels. I am going to ask God to lend me some wings, so I can go up and catch their pretty notes too; then I can sing like the little robins and mocking-birds."

" Oh, Minnie, do ask for some wings for me, too, won't you?" said Birdie.

But Minnie was over her poetic mood when Birdie asked the question, and commenced whipping poor pussey for not going to sleep like a good baby.

Minnie is a famous little rebel. You would think, to hear her talk sometimes, that the war was still

going on, and that she was commander-in-chief of the Southern forces. She says she don't care what the big people have done, she don't mean to give up as long as she lives.

She has two dolls, and one she calls Mary Rebelia and the other Rebelia Mary.

Little Minnie's father fell during the war, and this is why her heart is so constant to our lost cause; for between her and her father there was more than ordinary affection, and she says she must always be what her father was.

The last time she saw him was just before he fell. He had spent a short time with his family, and the night he went away he took little Minnie—previous to his departure—and sat alone with her before the fire-place. Little Minnie had her arms around his neck and her head on his shoulder, and as they both sat there the big tears ran silently down their faces. Then, when the father had gone, little Minnie sat motionless in the same spot for an hour.

The father and child were never together again, but they will be some day in heaven, and this is the only thought that comforts little Minnie.

Little Minnie's friends do not like her to feel so

bitter towards our enemies, and they try to make her feel differently; but whenever they say anything on the subject to her, she looks up wonderingly and says, " Do you forget my beautiful papa," then she goes away and says her prayers.

Now, little Minnie, like every one else, has a great respect for our noble General Lee. So the other day her auntie told her the following incident about him, hoping that it might teach her a good lesson :

Near the place where the General surrendered, a young lady lived, who was an intimate friend of his family. She saw all the proceedings of the surrender from her window, and became so excited that she rushed from the house, and throwing her arms about his neck, exclaimed, " Oh! General! General! has it come to this?" The noble old man looked at her for a moment, while the big tears rolled down his care-worn cheek; then uttered, in a clear but low tone, while he raised one hand to heaven, " Be reconciled, my child; the Supreme knows best." " Did General Lee say that?" said Minnie, when her auntie finished. " Yes," replied the auntie. " Well, then," said Minnie, " I will try to say so too; for he

14

is one of the noblest men God ever made. Bless his dear old heart!"

Now, one hot day last summer, Lutie, Birdie and Minnie, all began to tease their auntie to tell them stories; but their auntie did not feel well, and proposed that, in place of that, they should go in another room, and go to sleep, and try to dream; then, when they woke up, auntie would listen to their dreams, and write them down in a book for them, and give the book to Santa Claus, to sell for the benefit of some little Confederate children who had lost everything by the war.

" Oh, that will be so nice," said Birdie; " let us do it right away."

But Minnie, who had forgotten her good resolves already, said: " I don't want to give any of my dreams to Santa Claus, for he wasn't a rebel. I know he wasn't, for he never came to the Southern children for four Christmas Eves.

" How could he run the blockade ?" said Lutie.

" Oh, very well, if he wished to," said Minnie. If he can fly on to the tops of houses, and go over the whole world in one night, he could run any blockade. He is a mean old thing, and I don't like him."

15

"Perhaps he has some good excuse," said the
auntie. "We ought not to condemn him without
good reason. At any rate, dream your dreams, and we
will try and find out Santa Claus' principles afterward.

So the children all went off to go to sleep, except
Lutie, who stopped a moment and said : "Auntie,
sing me that little song about the goddess Flora, so I
can dream something pretty about her." And the
auntie complied, and sung the following lines to the
air of "Beautiful Venice" :

Beautiful flowers,
Growing in bowers,
Ye mind me of powers
    Mysterious, divine.
Are ye spirit or fay,
As ye spring from the clay,
In glorious array,
    Our thoughts to refine?

Has Flora a mine,
Of tintings so fine,
Whose beauties outshine
    Golden ore, deep in earth?

16

Does she limn ye all there,
So radiant, so fair,
To weave in our hair,
    In our summers of mirth?

From ye, wondrous things,
A lesson Hope sings
Unto me, and brings
    Serene Faith, while I think,
How like you I must die,
And in the ground lie,
Shut out from the sky,
    When my life's sun shall sink;

Yet again rise like ye,
But immortal to be,
My Saviour to see,
    On His throne in the skies;
If I bloom but aright,
In the garden so bright,
Of the gospel's pure light,
    My soul's germ, can not die.

"Thank you," said Lutie to her auntie; "now I
am sure I will dream about Flora. I do believe that

Birdie and Minnie are fast asleep, and they will get way ahead of me."

The little girls were not long gone, when they came back ready to tell their dreams. They all commenced speaking at once to their auntie, for even well-bred children do sometimes forget that it is bad manners to do so, when their little hearts are very eager. Their auntie, however, quieted them by saying, " One at a time, my dears; and Lutie first, as she is the oldest." Then she got out her pen and paper, and began to write down

LUTIE'S DREAM.

" Auntie," Lutie commenced, " do you know the high trunk of a tree in the front garden, which is covered all over with beautiful ivy ?" "Yes," replied the auntie. " Well," said Lutie, " I dreamed that Birdie, Minnie, and myself, were playing around it, and all of a sudden it opened and shut us up in itself.

" At first we were so frightened that we trembled all over; but presently we discovered a pure white marble staircase, leading downward into the earth. As soon as we saw it we were frightened no longer, and taking hold of each other's hands, we commenced going down the steps.

"All along the sides were beautiful flowers, and when we reached the foot there was a large room of crystal that shone like diamonds, and in the centre of it was a gold table covered with flowers and fruit. And Birdie and Minnie were so delighted that they shouted and danced and clapped their hands.

"And while they were doing this, we saw coming towards us from the lower end of the room, oh such a beautiful lady, with a wreath of pink roses on her head, and a garland around her neck, and she smiled very pleasantly on us. 'Oh,' said I, 'that is Flora, the goddess of flowers. I know it is.' And when the strange lady heard me say this, she bowed her head to us and said :

"'Yes, that is my name; and this is a portion of my spring and summer residence, to which I am very happy to welcome you.'

"'Is this the place where you make flowers?' said Minnie.

"'Yes,' she replied.

"'Please, lady, show us how you do it,' said Birdie. 'We'll be ever so good and quiet if you will,'

" 'Most of the flowers are made for this season,' said Flora; 'but I will gratify you to some extent. I will show you how I color them. Follow me.'

" Then the goddess Flora led us through other rooms like the one we were in, until she came to one that was covered all over the sides and roof with crystals that were every color that we ever see in flowers. Then, going up to a deep crimson tinted one, she tapped it gently with a rose-bud, and forth flowed into a cup she held, a liquid of the same color as the crystal.

" 'Now, little girls,' said Flora, 'are there not some white roses in your garden, just by your auntie's window?' 'Yes,' we all answered.

" 'Well,' said Flora, 'come with me, and we will go to that portion of my home that is just beneath those roses.'

" So we ran along by Flora's side, and presently we found ourselves in another crystal room, and looking up to the roof of it, we saw ever so many green and brown roots hanging through it. 'Those roots,' said Flora, 'are the roots of the flowers just around your auntie's window. Now watch me, and you will see how I turn the white roses red.'

" Then Flora glided up to the roof as if she had possessed wings, and hung the cup containing the crimson liquid so that the roots of the white rose-bush would be covered by it. Then coming down to us again, she said : ' Now, when you go home, look at the white rose-bush, and you will find that the flowers have become red, and be sure you do not tell any one how they came to be so, for this is your and my secret.'

" ' Oh, my,' said Birdie, ' I am so sorry I saw you do it, Miss Flora; for I never could keep a secret. I am sure I shall tell.'

" We thought the goddess would be vexed at Birdie for saying this, but she was not. She patted her on the head and smiled.

" ' Do you color all your flowers this way ?' said Minnie.

" ' Yes, little bright-eyes,' said the goddess. " I go all over the world doing it, and sometimes I am very tired. Then, when I see little children and idle persons destroying my flowers, it makes me very sad. I think little Minnie does this sometimes, doesn't she?'

" ' Yes, I do,' said Minnie ; ' but I won't any more, for I will think how hard you have to work.'

" ' Do you live in this place all alone, Miss Flora ?' said Birdie.

" ' Oh, no, I live with my flowers,' answered Flora, ' and they talk to me when we are by ourselves. I am never lonely with them. You cannot think what beautiful tales and legends some of them have to tell. If you come to see me again, I will tell you some of them. Then sometimes sly Cupid comes down here, but not to see me. He covers his arrows sometimes with my flowers. And I have two friends—Ceres and Pomona. Those were their fruits that you saw on the gold table in the first room you were in. Come and get some, for you must be hungry.'

" We were all so glad when the goddess said this, for we wanted some of the fruit so badly.

" So Flora took us to the room, and heaped up great piles of flowers for us to sit on. And what do you think Birdie did; she spoke right up and said :

" ' Miss Flora, I like meat a great deal better than fruit—have you got any ?' I was so ashamed of Birdie I did not know what to do, and I kept winking and nodding at her to stop, but she would not."

Then the goddess answered her and said :

" ' Meat!—what is that? I never heard of it.' And when Birdie told her what it was she was shocked.

" ' Oh!' she exclaimed, ' how dreadful to eat meat. If you would eat nothing but the nice fruits and vegetables that my friends Ceres and Pomona prepare, you would become like the goddesses.'

" ' Where are your friends?' said Minnie. ' Take us to see them.'

" ' No, not to-day, little dear,' said Flora. ' They are very busy preparing for their autumn work. They cannot see you. Besides, you must eat and go home; your auntie will be worried about you.' So, saying this, she gave Minnie a beautiful green plate that looked like a large leaf, and Birdie and me she gave some that seemed like large roses; and she heaped them up with delicious fruits. And all the time we were eating showers of violets and orange blossoms fell around us. When we had finished, she took us to the top of the marble staircase, and told us to knock three times on the old tree whenever we wanted to see her, and it would open and let us in. Then she kissed us all around, and glided to the foot of the steps without touching them. And when she got to the foot of them, what do you think bad little

Minnie did. Why, she called the kind goddess all the way back; and when she got there, she looked in her face and said : ' Goddess, are you a rebel ?' And before she could answer—I waked up."

" Oh, what a beautiful dream," said Birdie. " Let us go quick and knock on the old tree, and maybe it will all come true."

" Not so fast, not so fast, little Birdie," said the auntie. " You must tell your dream, and Minnie hers, before you can leave the room."

" My dream is funny and short," said Birdie, " and I hope Minnie's is too; for I am in such a hurry to look for the marble stair in the tree."

BIRDIE'S DREAM.

" I dreamed that it had been a very hot day, and that towards sunset we had a shower; and after the shower Lutie, Minnie and I walked to the top of the hill on the other side of the house. And just as we reached there, a beautiful rainbow came out of God's hand into the sky, and the end of the rainbow rested at the foot of the hill. And Minnie said :

" ' Let us all run down to the end of the rainbow, and find out what it is made of.'

"So, auntie, we ran down; and now guess what it was made of, sure enough."

"I cannot, I am sure," said the auntie. "You will have to tell me. Perhaps it was of different colored ribbons."

"No, no," said Birdie, laughing and clapping her hands, "it was all kinds of candy. The white was cream, the pink peppermint, the yellow lemon, and the purple chocolate; and when we found out it was candy we all commenced nibbling at it, just as hard as we could. We had a right good hold of it when we heard a sliding noise above us, and looking up, we saw the tiniest little lady, dressed in all the colors of the rainbow, coming down towards us on it; and Lutie cried out:

"'Oh, children, that is Iris, the goddess of the rainbow, and she will be so vexed with us.'

"And sure enough it was Iris; but just as she came near enough to scold us, I waked up—and that is my dream."

"Now, Minnie, you tell yours, and make haste, so we can go out to the old tree."

MINNIE'S DREAM.

"My dream," said little Minnie, "was sad and happy too. I dreamed our home was just as it used to be, even to all the pretty things in it, and my rocking horse and toy house. And my dear beautiful papa was there, laughing his big hearty laugh that made us all so merry. I thought papa and I had been playing in the new mown grass, until we were both so tired that we laid down in it and went to sleep. And in my sleep a dark, fierce-looking man stood over me, and said: 'Get up, little girl; you are too happy there with your father; get up and come with me.'

"I was frightened and did not want to go, but he made me. Then he seemed to take hold of me, and drag me by my arm into a dark cavern, in which was a big frame with a black curtain before it; and drawing the curtain aside, he said: 'Look in there, little girl, and see a part of your life.' And I looked, and saw a cold, dark ocean, and its great waves rolling right on to me; heavy black clouds almost met the waves, and the whole picture gave me a shuddering cold feeling all over, and I wanted to die.

"After that the fierce man seemed to take hold of

me very roughly, and to drag me down a steep precipice, from the sides of which came great balls of fire and awful green serpents; and the balls of fire kept shooting across my feet, and the serpents crawling in and out; and I screamed out: ' Oh, papa, papa, come and help me!'

" And when I called papa the fire and the snakes went away, and a holy light seemed to come out of the rocks and trees and sky; and looking up to see what made the beautiful light, I saw directly in front of me a great shining golden cross, and over it were beautiful angels, each holding a bright letter which spelt these words :

'Little Minnie, for thy only true refuge in life look thou here.'

"Then I waked up, auntie. But my dream has made me happier."

When little Minnie finished the dream, Lutie, Birdie and auntie had tears in their eyes, and the children had forgotten all about going out to the old tree to knock three times to see if it would be open. So then auntie commenced and told them many pretty stories about the sacred cross that Minnie had seen in her dream, which some day she hopes to write down too; and about our Lord who was crucified on it; how He loved little children, and watched over them especially.

"I don't think," said Lutie, "that we think half enough of the pain that dear Jesus suffered. Just think how we cry and fret if we only pinch ourselves, or prick ourselves with a pin, and poor Jesus had great nails driven through his sacred flesh; and just think of the long weary walk he took bearing a heavy cross on his shoulders, after he had been beaten until he was faint from it."

"Poor Jesus!—I am so sorry for Him," said Minnie. "Please don't talk about it, Lutie; it makes me cry."

"If you feel sorry for Him, dear children," said the auntie, "try and never offend Him; try to be as good as you know how; for sin and wickedness hurt Him a great deal more than the nails, the crown of thorns, or the weary walk."   *   *   *   *

"Auntie," said Birdie, "you had a funny dream once, in a steam car; it was all in rhyme, and imitated the locomotive; won't you put it in the Christmas book? It pleased us children, and I think it will please other little children. Please say it to us now, and please put it in the book."

LUTIE, BIRDIE AND MINNIE.

" Very well, Birdie. I will put it in," said the
auntie, " if you say so. But if the little girls and
boys don't like it, they must blame you and not me."

· SONG OF THE LOCOMOTIVE.

I commence to sing my ditty,
Starting from a slumbering city,
Ere I dive through tunnel darksome,
Made in labored hours irksome,
    And I puff, puff, as I go.

Crossing architectural bridges,
Spanning, to the very edges,
Rivers quickly rolling under ;
Still with roar and din of thunder,
    Puff I, puff I, as I go.

Now along a miry meadow,
Then through fields of corn, which shadow
Golden harvests, rich, abundant,
Garners full and barns redundant,
    Puff I, puff I, as I go.

Then again the landscape's broken,
And I see in distance token
Of the ocean's wavy mystery—
Who can tell its wondrous history—
    As I puffing, puffing go ?

LUTIE, BIRDIE AND MINNIE.

Glancing now through long plains dreary,
Passengers inside grow weary,
Look to travellers down the aisle,
Something must the mind beguile,
    As I puffing, puffing go.

What see they in all the faces,
Ticketed for different places?
See they joy, or love, or sorrow?
If they see, who'll care to-morrow,
    As I puffing, puffing go?

In the centre see that couple!
He, the man, tall, sinewy, supple;
By his side, with cheek all glowing,
Sits his bride, fond words bestowing,
    As I puffing, puffing go.

Look again in yon dark corner,
Think you not the man's a foreigner?
Why so restless is his eye
If you meet it passing by?
Shows he not a villain's face,
Flees he not from dire disgrace,
    As I puffing, puffing go?

Now all eyes again are viewing
Pictures panoramic moving,

LUTIE, BIRDIE AND MINNIE.

Mountains high, and silvery cascades,
Pitching o'er the rocky façades,
   As I puffing, puffing go.

Blue skies cloudless make all ponder
How an accident might sunder
Life from out each poor frail tenement,
Sending souls to yon clear firmament.
   As I puffing, puffing go.

Delving down from this sublimity,
Pass I with renewed rapidity
Many a pretty cottage door,
Out from which the urchins pour,
Waving me a glad salute,
The day's event to them, hoot, toot,
   As I puffing, puffing go.

Soon I'll reach bewildering city,
And methinks I'll close my ditty;
There I'll land joy, sin and sorrow,
To take .up the same to-morrow,
Plying e'er to be in season,
Without rhyme, but with good reason.
Science brought me richest dower,
When she gave me motive power,
And I'll puff her every hour,
   Puff, puff, puffing as I go.

When auntie finished the locomotive song, little Minnie jumped up and said :

" Auntie, oh, auntie, I have thought of something we children can do before we give the book to Santa Claus. Let us write to General Lee, and ask him if Santa was our friend; and if he says yes, then we will give him the book, for the little Confederate children. So the auntie sat down and wrote the following funny little letter to General Lee, at the children's dictation :

" DEAR GENERAL LEE :—We think you are the goodest man that ever lived, and our auntie says you will go right straight to heaven when you die; so we want to ask you a question, for we want to know the truth about it, and we know that you always speak the truth.

" Please tell us whether Santa Claus loves the little rebel children, for we think he don't; because he did not come to see us for four Christmas Eves.

" Auntie thinks you would not let him cross the lines, and we don't know how to find out unless we write and ask you.

" We all love you dearly, and we want to send you

something; but we have not any thing nice enough; we lost all our toys in the war. Birdie wants to send you one of our white kittens—the one with black ears; but auntie thinks maybe you don't like kittens.

"We say little prayers for you every night, dear General Lee, and ask God to make you ever so happy.

"Please let us know about Santa Claus as soon as you can; we want to know for something very, very, very particular; but we can't tell *even* you why until Christmas time, so please to excuse us.

Your little friends,

"LUTIE, BIRDIE AND MINNIE."

The above letter was sent the following day, and in about a week the answer was received:

"MY DEAR LITTLE FRIENDS:—I was very glad to receive your kind letter, and to know by it that I have the good wishes and prayers of three innocent little girls, named Lutie, Birdie and Minnie.

"I am very glad that you wrote about Santa Claus, for I am able to tell you all about him. I can assure you he is one of the best friends that the little

Southern girls have. You will understand this when
I explain to you the reason of his not coming to see
you for four years.

"The first Christmas Eve of the war I was walk-
ing up and down in the camp ground, when I thought
I heard a singular noise above my head; and on
looking to find out from whence it came, I saw the
queerest, funniest-looking little old fellow riding
along in a sleigh through the air. On closer inspec-
tion, he proved to be Santa Claus.

"'Halt! Halt!' I said; but at this the funny
fellow laughed, and did not seem inclined to obey, so
again I cried 'halt!' And he drove down to my side
with a sleigh full of toys.

"I was very sorry for him when I saw the dis-
appointed expression of his face when I told him he
could go no further South; and when he exclaimed,
'Oh, what will my little Southern children do!' I felt
more sorry, for I love little children to be happy, and
especially at Christmas. But of one thing I was
certain,—I *knew* my little friends would prefer me to do
my duty, rather than have all the toys in the world; so
I said: 'Santa Claus, take every one of the toys you
have back as far as Baltimore, sell them, and with

the money you get buy medicines, bandages, ointments and delicacies for our sick and wounded men; do it, and do it quickly—it will be all right with the children.' Then Santa Claus sprang into his sleigh, and putting his hand to his hat in true military style, said : ' I obey orders, General,' and away he went.

"Long before morning he came sweeping down into camp again, with not only every thing I had ordered, but with many other things that our poor soldiers needed. And every Christmas he took the toy money and did the same thing; and the soldiers and I blessed him, for he clothed and fed many a poor soul who otherwise would have been cold and hungry. Now, do you not consider him a good friend. I hold him in high respect, and trust you will always do the same.

"I should be pleased to hear from you again, my dear little girls, and I want you ever to consider me,

" Your true friend,

" GENERAL LEE."

"Hurrah ! hurrah ! hurrah !" cried all the children when their auntie finished the letter ; " hurrah !

Santa Claus is a splendid old fellow. And was not General Lee good, to think to do all that for the brave soldiers?

"Let us call our book 'General Lee and Santa Claus,' and let us say, 'God bless both forever!!'"

About

S T R A T F O R D   H A L L

This facsimile was printed from an 1867 copy of General Lee and Santa Claus that is part of the rare book collection in the Jessie Ball duPont Memorial Library located at the Stratford Hall Plantation. Stratford, the birthplace of General Robert E. Lee in 1807 and home to five generations of Lees, is situated on a high bluff overlooking the Potomac River. The large H-shaped house, dating from the late 1730s, sits surrounded by a complex of six original outbuildings on 1,670 acres in Virginia's historic Northern Neck.

In 1861, General Lee wrote his daughters from Savannah, Georgia, saying: " I am much pleased at your description of Stratford and your visit. It is endeared me by many recollections, and it has always been a great desire of my life to be able to purchase it. Now that we have no other home, and the one we so loved [Arlington] has been so foully polluted, the desire is stronger with me than ever." Again, two weeks later, he wrote to his wife: "In the absence of a home I wish I could purchase Stratford. That is the only other place that I could go to, now accessible to us, that would inspire me with feelings of pleasure and local love. You and the girls could remain there in quiet. It is a poor place but we could make enough cornbread and bacon for our support, and the girls could weave us clothes. I wonder if it is for sale and at how much." Unfortunately, Stratford was not for sale, so Lee was unable to realize his dream.

In 1929, the Robert E. Lee Memorial Association purchased the Stratford property and began restoring the building and gardens as a memorial to General Lee. Since that time, Stratford has been open to the public. A nonprofit organization committed to preservation, research, and education, the association depends on the generosity of a large number of supporters throughout the United States to fulfill its mission. The royalties received from the sale of General Lee and Santa Claus will go to preserving and maintaining the home that Lee remembered so fondly.

For further information about Stratford Hall Plantation, please call (804) 493-8038.